How To Be This Man

How
To Be
This
Man

The
Walter Pavlich
Memorial
Poetry
Anthology

Swan Scythe Press
2052 Calaveras Avenue
Davis, CA 95616-3021
http://www.swanscythe.com

Editor: Sandra McPherson
Associate Editor: Susan Kelly-DeWitt
Book Design: Eric Gudas
Cover Design: Mark Deamer
Cover Art: Nathan Oliveira, "Painted Painter," oil on canvas, 66" x 54", © 1989, 2003 by Nathan Oliveira. Collection of Mr. and Mrs. Joseph Oliveira, image courtesy of the John Natsoulas Gallery.

ISBN: 1-930454-18-X

The text of *How To Be This Man* is set in Meridien Roman, with titles set in Formata.

CONTENTS

Foreword

Walter Pavlich
1955-2002

On a summer day in 2002 my always young, always kind, and ever-funny husband and soul-mate left his loved ones without his presence—except for the present of his poems. That voice, written down, made me value all the more the poetic self-portraits, conscious or inadvertent, that we leave of ourselves. In honor of Walter, this collection brings together many men's evocations and invocations of maleness, boyhood, guyness, the days of men's lives. The men speak with range—one learns of life and art from Petrarch's rooms and another from repairs to a Mercedes or from evolution of primeval animals—yet somehow they also speak with one voice. I am grateful to all the authors who honored my husband's memory by sounding like themselves.

Thanks to editors Susan Kelly-DeWitt, Ryan Miller, Leon Wartinger, Alejandro Escudé, Virginia Robinson, and Eric Gudas; and to the dozens of readers over the years for the Swan Scythe Press annual chapbook contest, from which most of these poems were singled out, unbeknownst to their authors until this year. Heartfelt gratitude to the donors to the Walter Pavlich Memorial Prize Fund. Your gifts have made publication of this book possible.

Sandra McPherson

PUTTING APPLE SAUCE ON A MORTAGE
COMMAND AND DEMAND GADGETS OF R LAND
PUTTING YOUR HARNESS ON THE RIGHT HORSE
DONT GIVE YOUR SELF AWAY TOO CHEAP
THE CHEFS LIP WAS AS STIFF AS A NEW PAIR OF SHOES
IS THE BLOOD PRESSURE TOO HIGH FOR THE PURSE

HAVE A WHALEING TIME AWAY FROM THE SEA
YOU CAN HAVE WHAT THE EAR AND EYE PICKS UP
I-AM-OVER RIPE AND MOST OF ME HAS NOT BEEN PICKED
OLD AGE HAS YE SURROUNDED WITH SHADOWS OF DOUBT
WHEN HEAVY HANDS HOLD OUT ON LITTLE WORK
IT IS NO BIG SERVICE CHARGE ON WORRY
HANG MY OPINIONS ON YOUR WASH LINE

Lewis Smith

To be a man
means constant
revision like
correcting a writing.

—Chinese fortune cookie

Harold Johnson

At the Jackson Pollock Retrospective in L.A.

Blue Poles, a long painting, mute, manic, American,
its tilted blue members looking strong as rebar
in the chaos they dominate, halted me and legions
of others open-mouthed, as if watching a dangerous
and fantastic aerial performance. All afternoon
I jostled back and forth between giant spattered
canvases. Lacy layered violence in the black and green
masterpiece once bartered for psychiatric help
tore at my schoolish fears. I floated back to my aunt's house
electrified, dreaming those brilliant splashes and drippings
from the wounded alcoholic. But crashed against
the drunken ghost of Uncle George, Aunt Martha's husband,
a tense umber ferret who disappeared for years at a time,
periodically spotted by cousins in St. Louis,
Cleveland, Detroit, or Los Angeles.
        I'd seen him once in person, years ago, looking
depressed and blinky. Mother had a picture of him
in uniform, standing at parade rest outside some tar-
papered Negro barracks. Now here he was, popped up in my face
at Aunt Martha's house. She barely got out, "This is Harold,
Lou's boy. He—" before he leapt into his monologue
about the war: That he was alive because the general,
a southerner, had liked the Negro unit's cooking,
and thus he hadn't had to cook under fire at the front
after the hell of amphibious landing. But he hadn't escaped
shock or alcohol. He sat there rocking to the progress
of whiskey and war through his heart. An ill wind—
I fought to hang on to the lamppost of my painting dream.
He slapped me on the kneecap—"Do ya hear me, boy!"—
with the back of his hand. War blazed before
his bloodshot eyes, and his voice boiled into my ears.
        He created the whistle of incoming
mortars, uprooted orchards in torn black soil, innocent
windfall apples scattered like flung beads of red and yellow
paint under zinc-tasting smoke. Some boys from Alabama
got wasted in a jeep with a colored captain and a boy

from Memphis who could play the saxophone...boxes
with their names stacked in a corner of a chilly hangar.
He showed me how he used to prop his teeth open
with his dogtags to test the notch because he was sure
he was going to bite some o' that sombitchin' French dust—
"That's a long way from Yakima, aint it, boy," he yelled,
backhanding my knee and fuming the air till my eyes watered.
But that cracker general had liked his cooking and
he'd lived. "You don't think that's somethin'?" He tried
to shake his head into comprehension, shuddered, rocked,
and cursed me for not being a sport
like Virgil, my twin brother, who armed him
with a bottle whenever they met. Then he veered back
to the war, staring bug-eyed into France, blue lips worming,
grey hair frozen straight up like one sitting terrified,
piloting his gravebox.

MARVIN BELL

He Said To

crawl *toward* the machine guns
except to freeze
for explosions and flares.
It was still ninety degrees
at night in North Carolina,
August, rain and all.
The tracer bullets wanted
our asses, which we swore to keep
down, and the highlight
of this preposterous exercise
was finding myself in mud
and water during flares. I
hurried in the darkness—
over things and under things—
to reach the next black pool
in time, and once
I lay in the cool salve that
so suited all I had become
for two light-ups of the sky.
I took one inside and one
face of two watches I ruined
doing things like that,
and made a watch that works.
From the combat
infiltration course and
common sense, I made a man
to survive the Army, which means
that I made a man to survive
being a man.

ALEJANDRO JAVIER ESCUDÉ

from The Immigrant's Question

Argentina

Still in the dust, in nineteen-eighty one,
from head to toe I, mother said, was a ghost.
Beyond my father's mill for grinding rock
were the hills of Córdoba, tawny and robust.
Workers knew me as *el hijo del patrón*.
I waded the ground granite piles until
the sun gave word in breeze and shadow.
Father put me over a shoulder; a happy kid
spilled dust over mother's kitchen floor.
Father joked: "Would you like to make a bid
for this load?" Mother laughed, then ordered
us both outside the door. Dad's barbeque
cooked up the summer air. It was all I knew.

After the Country's Collapse

My father held his head with both his hands.
"We're going to California," Mother said.
Her eyes were dying lanterns grown too bright
before the going out. "We have to leave,
we have no choice," Father added in a voice
I'd never heard before, but would soon know.
Then I cried for my backyard eucalyptus.
I knew we couldn't take the tree with us,
so I put it in a tear, small enough to fly
within the belly of that great, orange plane.
I remember palms, my first chewing gum
and the sound of English, like cracking nuts,
but Spanish, my Spanish, was a breeze
on a dusty road...I hugged a strange family.

Finding Work

I went with Mom to clean the wealthy homes;
tree-lined, shady streets awaited me.
I climbed on private gyms, I found pine cones.
Not far away, the always sharp blue sea;
we'd take a walk when we were done there
when mother said the house had been easy.
I once brought a sea shell to my father,
who smiled, so tired, took the thing
into his hand and said: "one in a million,"
resting for a moment on the bed.
At night I'd hear his barter and dealing;
a room to add, but more common a toilet.
"Scoundrels!" he'd yell. "The price's a killing.
You first have to get robbed to make a living."

Father's Workers

Father was the *Patrón;* they were painters,
plumbers, or carpenters. Mornings
they'd wait for us at bus stops; they were
from Puebla, Mexico, or from *La Capital.*
At home father might slip into their accent,
a brilliant knack mother found horrendous.
"Don't talk like that," she'd say. "It's hideous."
"Dear love, this land was once all Mexican,"
Father would rejoin. Sometimes, on the job alone,
the workers would tease me about women.
"You've got a lot of *gringas,* huh?" one joked.
"But he doesn't know what to do with them,"
they'd laugh. "Shut up," I'd say. "I'm the boss!"
They never would, it's what I grew to love.

MG Roadster

Mom's boss told her to follow down the stairs.
And Mother put her broom aside and went.
In the garage was a covered MG roadster,
pearly white and in condition; almost mint.
"It's yours," the red-haired Irish-woman said.
"It's for you and your family...yes."
"I thought I was to wash it," Mother confessed
later. "But it was true, she gave it to us."
We sold it only after Father and I drove it
once down Venice Boulevard full speed.
I was sixteen, Father taught me how to shift.
It was a jewel, a smooth egg-like rocket steed
roaring us both through a city our own.
The car was proof enough we'd made a home.

Tango

The accordion begins nostalgic staccato
for Buenos Aires. It's Gardel's tango,
Father's favorite: *Mano a Mano*.
The violins, the crippling piano,
a story of lost love and solitude.
Father shakes and sings in tears
recalling through some interlude
the old city's subway stops. "The years,"
he says. "To think you were this big..."
An immigrant's unsolvable question
in his eye: "Do I belong to this?"
He smiles, makes a conductor's gesture,
prepares his chest, shakes his fist!
Almost *el fin*, the tango speeds
to its declarative end, and bleeds.

JEFFREY FRANKLIN

Julian Bream

for P.V.L.

When your hand lifted to bid that final chord
    Safe passage, you held us for the close
To silence, then took a crumpled hankie
    From your back pocket and wiped your nose

Just as I've seen old carpenters do,
    Using a rough, three-stroke motion.
I wondered then why you forsake
    Your restored, Baroque villa by the ocean

For a different hotel suite each evening,
    With hardly an accolade left to accrue,
Sufficient wealth, your younger self
    The only performer sure to outstrip you.

For one moment I inclined to think
    Of that great calling we call Art,
But then remembered another who,
    As they say of racehorses, has heart:

My stepfather, bald and stooped now too,
    Puts on a suit and drives to offices
Where quietness gathers round filed papers,
    Because that's what it is he does.

C. G. MACDONALD

First Edition

> The Poison of the Honey Bee
> Is the Artists Jealousy
> —William Blake

Drawn into Cody's—any bookstore
is magnet enough, but this half shrine,
half house of dear, illicit pleasure...
no more a student, lacking time
to browse where minutes more

become a day and cash spent. I enter
the garden, home, the liquid surge
of authors, titles, current words.
Wading the new releases, a rock
turns stonefish. Spreading shock

shoots from the clutching hand on her book.
No reviews had warned me. Stunned—
a common name, I think. I look,
my rival smiling wildly. No wonder.
Eight famous voices thunder

praise, "Evocative—transcendent
unforgettable—necessary."
When we were students, she had won
brass rings for all her digits. Very
jealous, I would vent

poison words into the ears
of other seething, unprized writers.
My title wordplay, "Anyone
But Her," though arch, now goes unsaid.
What, really, had she done

to me? Her book had briefly jarred
my stupor with a deep, triumphant
blast—"Look on my works, ye lazy..." She'd
applied her slender butt to the hard
chair of accomplishment,

I chose the recliner. Scanning key
pages—not as good as feared,
nor bad as hoped.
                              Some unkind glee
awaits months off in Walden's where
I find the book remaindered,

"Lousy legs, as always." (Petty.)
I lift it. Lighter this time. First
edition, much reduced, like me,
passed over. Hoping future works
redeem obscurity,

I take it home to age with other
firsts: a thrift store "Life with Father,"
a signed Thom Gunn. Can she still breathe,
wedged there between two meaty books
by Carver and Welty?

Ron Mohring

PGH Airport

It is not the red-faced man
wearing dirty Reeboks and matching Illinois State
T-shirt and shorts. It is not
the man in the lime polo shirt who grabs at his clip-on
pager. It is not the tall man
in the white shirt carrying a Faulkner novel who eyes me frankly
but does not stop to say hello.
Not the small Brazilian man with the black elastic band
wrapped around his head,
bright wire mouth guard gleaming. Not the loping man
in soft gray cowboy boots
and drooping black felt hat, though he's passed this spot four times.
Not the man in the leather shop
with heavy silver loops in his ear. Behind a row of video screens
announcing departures,
a pair of muscled legs. It is not the man attached.
It is neither of the mustached ones
in matching Pittsburgh T-shirts, nor the businessman
carrying his metal briefcase.
Not the bearded man with his cap turned backward who smiles
as I stare, though for a moment
I think it could be him. The flight attendant with perfect hair,
the Greek man in the cobalt shirt
listening to headphones, the Asian man in the yellow mesh
tank top, arms and chest fluid, solid:
none of these will deliver me. The Greek man bites his nails.
White socks bunched
at his ankles. Mole above his lip. He is so beautiful, I can't
                                                        understand
why no one has found him.

WALTER PAVLICH

Two Tongues

I let him lick my tongue
a little.
His a rough wing.
His eyes closed.
If we lick together
we catch like the teeth
of one benign zipper.
Loving neutered thing
furry boneyard.
One long muscle
with one small thought,
how much you
die each day.

LARRY MOFFI

Wolf Whistle

You hardly ever hear it anymore
but the wolf whistle was unmistakable
then, and turned heads, too.
It was Raymond Biochetti, who
I later learned served serious
time, wolf-whistling up a foxy thing
that turned out to be my mother
at the bus stop outside third
period math class of a childhood
as lost as any whistle. You may
not even know what I mean, or
if you do you probably haven't heard
it much. It's so out of fashion now,
so impolite.
                    The last time the great
wolf whistled was '79 and I was three
flights high on a scaffolding with
Robert Otis in Roxbury, and both of us
whistled into the sweet morning air
before it baked us, before a winch
unbuckled, floating us a moment,
no more, on whatever carried our
song to her. She looked up—what
harm?—and waved at two guys black
and white, tall and short, young
and older just trying to hang on.

JOSEPH DUEMER

Celestial Woman Undressed by a Monkey

Khajuraho region, Madya Pradesh; Chandella Period (A.D. 975-
1000); buff sandstone. Nelson-Atkins Museum of Art,
Kansas City.

1.
It is what I dream of & even monkeys
have dreams in our small but nimble brains.
We are not like dogs, who are not
permitted in the temple's sacred precincts.
Born believers, we worship as
easily as we see, though we
see only indistinctly at a distance.
My mind is simple but without

brutality & I live
in this dream—monkey that I am—of a woman
reaching behind her to unclasp her hair.
She has stood a long time in this stone guise—goddess
born from shadow where rainwater floods over
the lip of a cistern. My small face—

2.
though partly knocked away—beholds her:
seeing is one kind of believing. It
is my task to look at her for
you & I have grasped the garment made of air
& pulled it from her shoulders down to
where it gathers loosely about
her hips. What's left of my face grins up at her
& why not? Prayer is no respecter

of species. For her part, she
looks down at me but gestures toward the infinite
horizon of her shoulders. Celestial,
her breasts & navel are three stars on which the cosmos
is founded. She is older than the idea
of God—a body for a primate's gaze.

ERIC GUDAS

The Bells

Outside of the church their tolling
stilled me, pure tones struck
in the fall air over
and around me. I stood as if in-
side the bell
of the bells, stomach of the hum
as it washed over the gritty
inner-iron, becoming membrane
of that sound. As when you rode
above me in bed, deital
eye of your cervix scraping me, not
peacefully: I held on while your pelvis
bucked, I felt I was and was not
the clapper of your bell—I felt we
were the bell, round ridged texture
of the outer trajectoral limits of your body clanging
against me. Whether I was screaming
or you were screaming, whether the blood
was yours or mine, the trace elements
of what we were
together marked that room, cotton
grid of the sheets, hard stucco of the walls: love's own
sanctuary, the two of us
kneeling as we knelled.

LEE BLESSING

from Thief River

RAY
(to audience)

The first time, I wasn't drunk. It wasn't 'way late at night. I wasn't
scared. It was my idea. Gil would never have suggested it. He
probably thought he was lucky out of his mind just to have
somebody to confide in. Confess to, more like it. I had to lie and
tell him I had a cousin who was queer, so he'd trust me enough.
Not that he'd ever done anything with anybody. But you know,
he had all these fantasies about everyone and stuff. I was the first
he ever told. We spent a whole afternoon on a rock by the river,
him telling me all this dirty stuff. Only it wasn't dirty. It was just
like how gorgeous he thought these stupid football players were. I
just kept listening to him. That afternoon, and the next and the
next...
(A beat)
That's how you fall in love. One confession at a time.

(RAY exits. Action continues as lights crossfade)

ANY NUMBER BECOMES 1 | WEEDS IN LAZY MANS GARDEN

WHAT DOTH DEATH GAIN | BE YOUR OWN BELL HOP

GOOD SELLS EASY | SUGAR IN R TAY

SUN GLASSES 4 BATS | ADD A PINT TO YOUR EXHAUST

WHAT YOU MISS WILL CARRY WELL

I WANT WHATS IN THAT SONG

NEWSPAPER TELL TIME OF DAY

IN THE OUTLINER INN

R.T.O.K. = KISS KILL - GO T.V.

TACTICS OF LIFE IS A BIG BUNDLE

DEAF MAY PAY DIVIDENTS

BAD LUCK AT CLOSE RANGE

IN MY SPARE TIME I THINK OF ME

FISHING NOT FOR FISH | I HAVE HORSES TO HOLD

GREEN HORN SEE LONG HORN | EXPOSED FOOLISHNESS FLORISHES

SACK YOUR OWN WHEAT | WILD OATS ON CAMPUS GREW

FOOLS COME WHOLESALE | GALVANISED SUGAR

Lewis Smith

JACK RIDL

The Man Who Wants to Change the World

He wonders if exchanging the names
would help. Suddenly no one could say
"monkey" in the same old way. You
would have to pause, say, "What's
the new name again? Oh, yes,
sassafras." Or you would be told,
"Give me the wisteria to your riverbed,"
or find yourself asking, "Why don't we add
some whispers to the armoire or to the truck?"
He realized this one hazy afternoon
when staring up through the trees' wild
acceptance of their branches' tangle,
he noticed how the light settled
along the leaves. He wished the robins,
vireos, nuthatches, and catbirds could see it.
And that night he wondered all the more
when, drying the plate from his small dinner,
he felt everything around him leaving, felt
himself left amidst the sparks of dust floating
across the window. That night he sealed and
stamped empty envelopes to send to everyone
he loved. The next morning he began making
a list of words: bread dough, lightning, salt,
candle, mourning dove, tunnel. He thought
if he exchanged them for last laugh, coffin,
profit margin, proliferation, knife, computer,
they might lead those lost in the language
to wander along, maybe look at the sky.

GEORGE VAHLE

Eight-Year-Old Boy Sees

Her comb slips off the vanity.
When she bends,
I see an open wound between her legs.
Notice a swelling in my groin
that grows like a lip stung.
I want to show it to her.
Holding my penis I say *mom, look.*
At bedtime she reads from Leviticus:
...the nakedness of thy mother,
shalt thou not uncover...
I smell the dust on the Bible, the thickness
of sex on my fingers, a sweetness
between my legs. Say nothing.
And when she turns out the light
and shuts the door,
I am left in the darkness,
where no one can see me
looking like a man.

Fishing the Klamath River, 1953

The father a fish, is the rumor among friends,
some great-finned river god up from the sea,
gone dark, losing its iridescence between her legs.
Downstream, an old Yurok dies laughing, mouth agape.

I float down spring's amniotic streams,
dreaming of the great blue branching,
watching blood stars fall in the darkness
the tide merciful beside her leviathan heart.

As my father builds his kayak, gills,
then the web between my toes disappear.
I listen to every promise ever made between lovers,
the vow never to leave as they were left.

But, even now, in the shade of my mother's breath,
angry blood knots in me,
as rising to the light,
water breaking, hands
like eagles come for me.

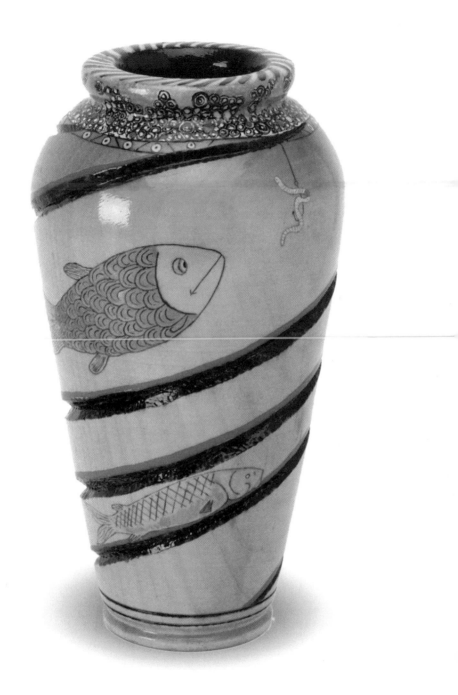

Jerry Matzen

JOHN ALLEN CANN

Memories

There's a trilobite in my foot,
mellow whenever in river shallows
or sliding in sea-foam,
and from my knees
I'm getting this picture of a huge dragonfly
cruising ancient riverbanks
beneath thick conifers.
Molecules near my elbow
are transmitting
the image of something crocodilian,
armored from snout to tail,
secretive & savage
in shadowed waterways.

Now I'm feeling a twinge in my neck
like a pterosaur lifting off a cliff,
sailing a wind out to sea,
and in my left brain
Deinonychus dances through ferns,
while in my right,
Ultrasaurus
chomps on a whole forest.

My third eye
reconfigures the tan smilodon
waiting by a tar pit
ready to lunch on a sinking mastodon,
and the flightless dodo
peeks
out of my heart.

WALTER PAVLICH

How To Be This Man

Stop a neighbor boy from aiming at crows with his
slingshot at the park.

Help to carry a man out in full seizure from the back of
a church.

Appreciate "characters" of all types. So the loop running
through my mind is your refrain, "Walt, all I know
is characters." Which applies to "character actors."
So I can identify Ward Bond in any old movie he's
in. Talk with inmates in common brotherhood.
Know that anywhere I go some character is always
waiting to be recognized, has stories to tell, feels
both appreciated and underappreciated at the same
time and has learned to live with that. Mailman,
teller counting out change, the person in the corner
of any room who waits and waits for a chance to
tell everything they know.

Razz with the best of them. The delicate nature of
kidding someone just right. A currency so much
more important than money that I've learned to
exchange with almost anyone.

Pick up a shot and a beer and tell a boozy truth.

Sit and listen to others tell how to put that shot and beer
down and live sober.

How to get up morning after morning year after year in
the dark and drive to the shop and listen to the
machines fire up.

Watch a boy being brought in to our grade school on a
handtruck by his father because they couldn't
afford a wheelchair and take that lesson in and use it for
the rest of my life.

Have fun before during and after a funeral.

Sulk in a room alone in resentment, drawing the
curtains on a wife.

Try to prevent mistakes you've already made.

Learn that each morning is essentially a clean slate like
a blackboard only partially erased.

Wear a paper sack hat while cleaning out the fireplace.
Pick glass out of a dropped peanut butter jar and
then make a sandwich. Pay strict attention to the
tectonic plates of your bowels. Drive to the hospital
with metal slivers in your forearm. Fall down a
flight of stairs at age eighty, come to in the
ambulance, ask, "Who's paying for this ride?"

Turn down a hearing aid to save money on batteries.
But listen, listen always. Because the world is
talking.

W. JOE HOPPE

Sanding Floors

Caught between agriculture and industry
I tread grained rows
I grind up golden dust
triceps flexed and small of back strained
behind a tumbling drum sander
a silver juggernaut with blue sparking motor
ravenous teeth on a roll under my control
short leashed it grumbles
I follow in cloudy plastic goggles
black rubber respirator a filtered trunk
like an elephant headed deity of the hearth
like an astronaut harvesting the moon
I scour these oaken floors with gravity
36 Grit
Like lamprey's teeth on a steel cylinder
to gouge and tear in long splinters
through the black carpet backing
through the ancient dried glue
through the glaring waxed finish
I grind on through these old boards' tattoos
60 Grit
More precious now
like a granddad's whiskered cheek
to a goodnight kiss
spun round to ride the channeled waves
knocking off their curls their
whitecaps churned beneath
harnessed horses' hooves and teeth
to flow soft upon the floory shore
100 Grit
Sharkskin smooth for a final run
amber waves of grain all raised
a heightened vibrancy arises
heart's secrets brought up to the surface
with democratic leveling to stand
equal individual and nakedly alive

I walk these planks in noise and dust
to make a home out of this house
I am the reaper of rough
I am the sower of smooth

David Salner

The Machinist and the Cell Phone

Entering the machine shop was not like entering hell
or a prison—more like a night without sleep,
a few hand-cuts and metal splinters, a cold wind
under the steel roof with its I-beams and angle rafters,
the smell of the coolant, and the sound
of compressed air whistling in tapped holes
all midnight shift. And then there was Harry,
who ran the horizontal mills, his bald head
gleaming like milled aluminum, his face bright
from grandstanding beside his machine and telling stupid jokes
we had to laugh at—he was part of the sentence.

One shift I saw a phone in Harry's box, a cell phone,
beside the mics and dial calipers, which he kept safe,
like jewelry, on green felt. The phone lit up like an icon
waiting to be clicked, so I said: "Harry, what's a machinist
doing with a cell phone in his box—is it
for dealing drugs or trading stocks?" I pushed
my face into his. My words gleamed like a ground tool
between us. His face dulled as he told me
his son would be out plowing snow
from the county roads all night. "That leaves his mother
alone, and she has cancer...She might need someone
to talk her through the pain."

The mills howled, putting their fearful shine on everything.
I don't remember what I said, but Harry said, "That's o.k."
I sat down to a bin of parts that needed deburring, feeling like
                                        a prisoner
who wanted himself—more than his sentence—to disappear.

Even before I heard the ring, Harry was reaching
into his box, saying into his phone: "I'm here."

GENE EPSTEIN

Subway Worker in Bronx Kills Colleague and Himself

John O'Brien stuttered said a neighbor
And they made fun of him at work, not
That he seemed the type who would
Shoot someone for doing only that. No,
He was a tall, gentle kind of guy who
Appreciated nature, the birds, the feel
Of the place here by the sea, who kept to himself...

Like O'Brien, I too suffer this affliction
Known to every language, it's supposed, since
Talk began. Not perhaps as shackled as he
But having the words emerge in spasms ("He
Stuttered like an idiot," wrote Dame Edith Sitwell)
When I, the new boy in a new school in
A new city, was asked to tell all those
New faces looking to find fault my name,
So that speaking became the thing
I could not do. I was of course derided
But only until I rushed at them with
My fists and thereby introduced myself.
(Animals can't talk, but they can bite.)

This solution was evidently not O'Brien's,
Though to be sure this was not a schoolroom
But a yardshed in the Bronx past which
The subway runs, a job with benefits that
You tell yourself you'd be crazy to quit,
So that miserably you report in until
The day when you decide your only
Chance for completion is with a gun.

So let's say another train has passed and it's
Momentarily quiet and you speak your piece.
This time you're heard without the mean
Laughter tearing through your chest.
This time, for once, you're fluent.

ARTHUR HEEHLER

I'm a Bureaucrat Translating Agricultural Policy

I travel calming the hidden fears of farmers.
Photos of me kneeling on the black soil of Africa
stroking the coiled beard of a goat
bring herdsmen together.

I turn to a Masai
during a Millet Convention in Cairo
holding my calabash thoughtfully.
A camera person circles
catching the compassion I share
with the Nile.

I flood newsletters in Nebraska
soliciting a return to the mortar
and pestle.

A photographer captures me outside Peking
behind two oxen trying to breed.
The photo is a triumph
and works its way
into a discourse on the Work Ethic in Cincinnati.
An infatuation with hooves dominates my leisure.

Again by foot across range land south into New Mexico.
I take up ritual and tobacco. In Taos I romance
the red earth of the Dirty Thirties.

On windy nights I lose myself. I travel on foot
between countries. I cross oceans on ships
importing soil inside the false bottom
of my sole.

JOHN OLIVARES ESPINOZA

Father's Way of Getting His Jobs Done

Father scolds us at home because that's his second job.
   At his first job, he scolds his workers. They seem slow:
   Hands cramped from too much pruning.
Thigh and calf muscles feel like egg whites
Pouring down from a puncture in the shell.
The sun drains their energy like a child sucking on flavored ice.
Father gets paid to yell louder than the machinery.
   But at his second job, it's completely on a
                voluntary basis.

   Then he brought us to work with him and scolded
   Us some more. He just couldn't get enough.
Scolded us for leaning on the rake for support,
      As leaves rested unraked—each one a wish
   To be stretched across a velvet sofa asleep,
   Dreaming about the weight of teenage breasts
Measured on the scale of our hands.
Scolded us for not knowing the names of tools
   In Spanish, though we didn't know them in English—
   Each one a mouth chomping on PVC pipes,
      Without a word to say to any one of us.
Father liked his sons to be like his pliers.

Scolded for asking too many questions at home,
   We hid away in our room with three beds,
Rushed through our homework, played video games—
   The volume hushed like mutterings during deep sleep,
      As not to compete with the sounds of passionate
         Embraces during my parents' telenovelas.
   When we stepped out, it was only for a cold drink.
   Barefoot on the tile, we were scolded again
Because walking without slippers
And drinking cold water would get us sick.
   "Do I have to tell you each and every time?" he'd say.
   This was his mission statement.

No matter how many times I was lectured,
I don't remember the face.
Just the voice, a knife in the eardrums.
I remember the swollen chest, the shoulders
                    Looming over me like mountains
            Wearing a green flannel shirt.
    If we talked back, he'd crush us
Like a beer can under his boot treads.
    He was the Big Bad Wolf in a sombrero and mustache.

            (Memory, 11 years old:
        The front yard smells of orange blossoms.
We wrestle with Dad, one is a necklace,
    With his arms flexed, two sons
            Hang on as if they're swinging from a branch.)

                I turn 21, convinced I'm a man myself,
            Came home from college,
    Found myself taller than my father,
And I realize two things:
Perhaps Dad isn't such a bad guy after all?
    With two degrees at my side,
        He rebuked the lazy soul out of me.
            And he was never big to begin with.
Was it because I hadn't grown yet, I wonder?
    Or because my head always looked downward,
            Too ashamed to look him in the eye?
        He looks up at me now, all smiles
"What a fine job I've done with you."

RON MOHRING

Windows

Because I didn't know exactly what I was doing, I succeeded.

Because I have a homo sensibility, and thought: Well that
                                        looks nice
but what if I started with much smaller pieces?

Because for months on end I never picked it up, it's still
                                        unfinished.

One-inch squares cut from every fabric I could find.
Framed by scalloped muslin folds. The tiny stitches I learned
                                        to make.
The muslin blocks vary in shade and texture, at least four kinds,
because I didn't know how much I'd need.

Take a four-inch square of unbleached muslin. Press in half.
Stitch an eighth-inch seam along both narrow ends.

Mother's yellow kitchen curtains. My sister Jenny's handmade
                                        dress.
A bag of vintage scraps sent by my now-dead aunt, horrid
clashing patterns, wild smears clipped and squared, made tame
by simple reduction. Everything goes in and all of it belongs.

At first, the challenge of not repeating a single fabric pattern.
Then the math: impossible to count, keep track. Impossible to
                                        find
that many samples, though Mother saved dozens, sent them
                                        in batches
through the mail, a short note and a tumble of scraps inside a
                                        squashy envelope.

Pull open the rectangle so it purses along the unstitched sides
and the seams meet at a middle point. Line up the raw edges.
Stitch a seam two-thirds their length from each end,
leaving the middle unsewn.

At a quilt shop, Mother brags about my project. The owner
                              bristles:
But it's not a true quilt. There's no batting, and no quilting to speak of.
It should truly be called a <u>coverlet</u>. Yes, I nod. But want to say
Lady, who gives a shit?

Because it was something to do with my hands
on the airplane, in the waiting rooms, in the vinyl hospital
                              chair.
Watching David sleep. The gooseneck lamp casting enough
                              light to work by,
the basket of scraps in my lap. Stitching. Folding. Thinking:
He is dying and this is all I know to do.

Turn the piece inside out and smooth the seams. You should have a
                              square.
Whipstitch the center closed. Now bring one corner point
to the center and tack with two small stitches. Repeat for the other three
                              corners.
You will need to make hundreds of these.

The flight attendant, the receptionist, a small boy in the
                              hospital
waiting room: *What are you making? May I see?* And I thought: I
                              am a man
who sews in public. Not as performance, and despite my fear
                              of ridicule.
I find my seat on the bus, in the auditorium, and I pull out
                              my sewing.

Sewing. Quilting. Piecework. Salvage.

Fold two blocks so the X's meet, and stitch them together
                              along one side. Open.
The intersecting triangles now form a diamond. Place a one-
                              inch square

44

of any fabric into this diamond. Fold one side of the diamond
                    so it laps
over the inset square's edge, and stitch in place. Repeat with
                    the other three sides.
This is the finished window.

Because nothing planned is random. I tried to use whatever
                    square
I'd pull next from the basket. Two reds. Green gingham then
                    blue gingham
then three blocks down the same green. But the patterns, the
                    colors
set up their own dialogue. The crimson from one piece
called to the gray pinstripe in the next. Flecks of that same gray
in a blue-green floral. Conjunctions. Associations.
Constellations in an unbleached field.

At the fabric store, Mother's friends ask: *Is he still working on*
                    that quilt?

Because I could not throw them away: David's shirts, the
                    buttons clipped off
and saved in a porcelain box, the sleeves removed so I would
                    never try
to wear them again, would have to cut them up for
                    something useful.

The quilt grew too large to carry. I hit upon the notion of
                    piecing strips,
two blocks wide and however many long I needed next, the
                    way you'd mow
a lawn by starting with a central square, zipping off one side,
                    quarter-turning
down the next adjacent row. But adding on, two blocks too long,
so each completed side begins the next, a spiraling path.
The first time I used solid black. The day he died

stitched in white. Such tiny numbers.

A six-block square section contains 60 inserts. If the finished
size is 48 blocks
square, it will hold two thousand five hundred and twelve
inserts.

Because I'm forty now.

Elegy. Anniversary. Silk ties, Christmas ribbon, underwear,
a napkin. Mother made a quilt, saved scraps for mine.
Bow Tie. Cathedral Window. Like separate animals
with shared chromosomes. Like windows in adjacent houses.

Because I want to finish it. And yet how satisfying to
complete each strip,
drape it over the back of a chair, see how much I've done.
I spend an hour a day on this, sometimes more. My new lover
drives the car,
everywhere we go so I can quilt.

Because nothing else I've done has felt so wholly mine.

ADAM SOLDOFSKY

The Life of a Suit

In walked a grieving widow
one slow Monday morning
to find a suit for her husband,
after years of punctuality, late.

Those were her words;
because when he was alive
he drove a truck across country,
sometimes all night to insure

his arrival at the freight dock
before breakfast. She explained
how he admired the well-dressed men
of classic cinema, and how he

mentioned every now and then,
how much he would enjoy
owning a tailor-made suit one day,
if only he could find a reason.

That is why she found her way
into the tailor's tidy shop,
her husband's measurements
scrolled across the reverse side

of a supermarket receipt,
and an old post card he sent her
from the road, with Humphrey Bogart
posed in a dinner suit behind the gloss.

And the tailor accepted,
pledged he could reproduce that suit,
because he was very good at his job
and he was a business man before all.

He laid out the materials,
measuring tape swinging from his neck,
cursing department stores for
marking up low end fabrics

on their so called designer outfits.
Soon the trousers took shape,
pleated much the way he wore his own,
and not one loose black string

hanging from their hem-lines.
He began the blazer, double breasted,
four buttons at the sleeve,
a pocket for a handkerchief.

He chose the shirt, the black tie, the belt,
the black shoes, arranging them
on the faceless mannequin,
smug if given the privilege of expression.

And he waited for the work day to end,
glancing at the suit now and then,
thinking about the man to whom
it would belong, how he would never

get his final fitting, how the ensemble
would deteriorate over time,
tearing with the skin, never to be
worn in the winter wind,

the jacket, never to be draped
over the shoulders of a woman.
Then, he phoned his wife at home,
made plans to meet for dinner.

He removed the pants and swapped
them with his own, they fit him fine
without alteration. Next the shirt and tie,
the black shoes, the flawless cream coat.

He closed his little shop,
went to dinner with his wife,
minding the merlot for sake of stains.
They went out dancing on a Monday night,

returning late in the evening,
his poor wife worn out from
the waltzing and the wine.
He hung that suit in his own closet

near a nice herringbone.
He wanted his suit to have a life,
to be creased at all the joints,
if only once before the wrinkling of repose.

In a day's time the widow returned,
cried when he revealed the suit, pristine,
pressed, the price reduced to half its worth;
it was only fair.

MARVIN BELL

The Uniform

Of the sleeves, I remember their weight, like wet wool,
on my arms, and the empty ends which hung past my hands.
Of the body of the shirt, I remember the large buttons
and larger buttonholes, which made a rack of wheels
down my chest and could not be quickly unbuttoned.
Of the collar, I remember its thickness without starch,
by which it lay against my clavicle without moving.
Of my trousers, the same—heavy, bulky, slow to give
for a leg, a crowded feeling, a molasses to walk in.
Of my boots, I remember the brittle soles, of a material
that had not been made love to by any natural substance,
and the laces: ropes to make prisoners of my feet.
Of the helmet, I remember the webbed, inner liner,
a brittle plastic underwear on which wobbled
the crushing steel pot then strapped at the chin.
Of the mortar, I remember the mortar plate,
heavy enough to kill by weight, which I carried by rope.
Of the machine gun, I remember the way it fit
behind my head and across my shoulder blades
as I carried it, or, to be precise, as it rode me.
Of tactics, I remember the likelihood of shooting
the wrong man, the weight of the rifle bolt, the difficulty
of loading while prone, the shock of noise.
For earplugs, some used cigarette filters or toilet paper.
I don't hear well now, for a man of my age,
and the doctor says my ears were damaged and asks
if I was in the Army, and of course I was but then
a wounded eardrum wasn't much in the scheme.

ADAM SOLDOFSKY

The Male Pattern

It could happen,
one morning I might look
to the mirror for solace and instead
discover something quite different—
an emerging pattern,

hairs abandoning their roots.
A few stragglers may remain
attached the vast acreage
that I once thought to be
very stylish space,

but most of them I imagine
will have gone by then, south,
in the great hair migration.
Some may settle early,
for and on my face.

I can see now why this is potentially
a very cosmopolitan plot.
Who knows, a sophisticated beard
could spring up from the industry
of my pores, becoming a great center

of progress and art.
Surely some will crave open space,
electing to set stake on
the rolling hills of my shoulders or
the prairie plains of my back.

A simple existence really,
out of reach from the hustle
and bustle of grooming,
ideal for those who want only
to be left alone.

And some may venture beyond,
to the buttocks, or along a leg,
scaling knee and shin and further still
until each lot has relocated
to a more ideal spot on the body—

the quiet knuckle of a toe perhaps.
But not all will share the same success—
some could indeed lose their way
overextending onto brush bristles,
coming up short in a sink or shower drain,

or just slipping through the hands,
filament and fiber
until nothing remains but
the vacancy that once was a crew-cut.
How hard it is to be a man—

how so much involved
promises to end a moniker for modesty.
How great it was to be a boy,
when everything remained
where it was the night before.

JOHN OLIVARES ESPINOZA

Humble Body

My torso, a visible network of bone,
    No muscle in sight.
The flab of beer, ham and cheese on white bread
Circles the navel like Saturn's rings.
            Shoulders, a diving board narrow.
            Hips the width of a cereal box.
As the Greeks did to their skies
During their starry summers,
Someone once connected the moles on my back,
    Forming the constellation of Hercules.

                *   *   *

            Though my arms appear thin
Enough to shatter mid-way a set of push-ups,
My biceps are oranges covered in flesh.
        Darker skin from the elbow down;
        It's not a farmer's tan, it's a gardener's,
After summer months of mowing and raking
In T-shirts from the previous school year,
Whose tears and holes have me looking back,
            Holding on to nothing.

                *   *   *

        I've seen men my age
Whose arms are bigger than my legs.
My legs hide beneath thick curls of hair.
The knees protrude like two Arizona mesas
        When I lie down,
But dissolve when I kneel on a pew,
As I offer a prayer to God to make these two miserable
        Appendages
Thick as the trunks of palo verde.

53

*   *   *

My feet are tiny, 8 or 8½
   Against the measurement of the shoe.
   Their calluses like turtle skin,
   Built up from steel-toe workboots,
Are finally beginning to wear
   As thin as a fallen maple leaf.
      Toenails clouded with fungus,
From wearing those boots all day,
Have now been swept away
      By the wind of modern chemistry.
Even with the grace and speed of Mercury's wings
   Donned on my ankles, these feet
      Couldn't outrun the oldest greyhound.

*   *   *

Cheeks scarred by scratching and picking
      High school acne,
As if struck by the thorns of a lemon branch.
   My ears stick out like satellite dishes
   Casting shadows of their own
   As I walk down a sidewalk at high noon.
My nose—a question mark tracing back to Zapata,
Who opposed the state at every turn.
Left eye out of focus because of a slight astigmatism
   Blurs the grace of the world
Making the orange blossoms of La Quinta
   Appear like desert snow.
      Yellow teeth stained by years
      Of the dark sips of Coca-Cola,
Straightened by metal brackets and wires,
Now shifted slightly out of place once again,
   Like pebbles in a Mojave wind.
I like my hair—before it grays like a December sky.

*　　*　　*

My heart settles comfortably in my chest
　　Waiting for the wisdom
Of fatherhood, age, and a steady check.
　　Waiting for clogged arteries
Or Angina Pectoris.
It is small and frail like a sparrow,
　　But it is kind
And pumping ever so solemnly.

JOSEPH GREEN

Among the Potshards

When he climbed the hill
where the ancient city had been,
he didn't know what to expect
so he didn't expect anything. Certainly not
a cistern dug into the top, long ago gone dry,
its plastered stone walls finally caving in.
The ground around it littered with bits
of crockery. Ordinary lives.
Ambitions spilling. Plans failing.
Dreams seeping out through the cracks.
He picked up a shard from the lip of a water jar.
None of the other fragments appeared to match it.
Then he knew with these people he would have been
the same as he was at that moment. Wanting
to remain completely alone and whole.
Wishing he could go to pieces, even so.

Arthur Ginsberg

After Jack's Heart Attack

he lay on crisp, white sheets, hallucinating
bicycle wheels, how each revolution
must come from the injured sack, sheltering
behind ramparts of ribs. Care-givers' voices
grew loud, then faded like childrens', playing
tag in a forest. *Capture the Flag* had been
one of his favorite games. Pablum passed
like prayers between lips. He thought this was
heavenly and forgot texture of meat; predatory
instincts edged away to some archetypal niche.
Breathing became sprint, he recalled a cinder track
where lungs quit down the stretch and knees
pounded on like an automaton, as if, they no longer
required blessed sacrament of air. Toward the end,

doctors spread his chest, glued a patch to the pump,
to revive this dying horse. Wire sutures trussed him
together like a Thanksgiving bird. Wrist and ankle
restraints, he imagined as bracelets suspended by
pulleys from the ceiling. At night, these lifted him
into air where he swam weightlessly, flitted brilliant
as firefly between hard shafts of surgical steel. When

that battered fist of muscle called heart, finally ground
to a halt, he was soaring through the forest, bathed
in mosaic columns of light, unaware of the crashcart's
shock, listening to the whole universe call his name.

FRANCISCO ARAGÓN

The Slide

Those twin cement flumes
at Seward Park, just
below Kite Hill: knob

on the city's heart swaying
with fennel and grass;
and the one fir

jostling with the wind whipping
down from Twin Peaks.
The patchwork of the city

starts at my feet, reaching
the wide stitch of the bay,
and across it a friend

and his fever, his cough. Late
afternoons that July:
a bench, a view, the air

moving through the trees, men
trailing dogs out
for a piss, the smells.

And heading home one night
along a different path
I happen on those

companion slides: grassy slope
of that narrow
street park beside the base

of Kite Hill, secluded
between houses and pine—that space
those years: me and Mick

adjusting the sheets of wax paper
we'd tear off and slip
under us, perched and ready

at the top...then down
racing over the hump mid-way
and down again...spilling

over the lip of our chute—
both of us in the end
sprawled in the sand.

San Francisco

EDUARDO C. CORRAL

Acquired Immune Deficiency Syndrome

I approach a harp
    abandoned
in a harvested field.
    A deer leaps
out of the brush
    and follows me

in the rain, a scarlet
    snake wound
in its dark antlers.
    My fingers
curled around a shard
    of glass—

it's like holding the hand
    of a child.
I'll cut the harp strings
    for my mandolin,
use the frame as a window
    in a chapel
yet to be built. I'll scrape

    off its blue
lacquer, melt the flakes
    down with
a candle and ladle
    and paint
the inner curve
    of my soup bowl.

The deer passes me.
    I lower my head,
stick out my tongue
    to taste
the honey smeared
    on its hind leg.

60

In the field's center
   I crouch near
a boulder engraved
   with a number
and stare at a gazelle's
   blue ghost,
the rain falling through it.

Adrian C. Louis

Goggles as Savior of Gizzard

One day I'm shuffling across campus, late for class, when the music begins. It's the saddest, bad-ass redskin blues you ever heard and only I can hear it. Every step I take is choreographed. Every step is strong and smiling. And as if my brain hadn't slopped enough cruel gruel onto my plate, I've now started to contemplate death and dying on a daily basis. *Lord, don't pity the poor poet and the sad and peculiar perks of his middle age. Death (and those fixations thereof) is in the first paragraph of his job description.*

My scenarios of demise dance to and fro, but seriously shake a leg when I remind myself that there's not a single student of mine born before the fall of Saigon. Nary a one who could explain the whys and wherefores of Huey P. Newton. And it's not like I really know when or how I will end and I guess I don't really care as long as I'm marching to a solid blues beat. Maybe, one fine day I'll be strolling to class in a blizzard when the big one hits like a ten-pound sledge to the chest. Whether I croak or just get deveined, I'll have no worries because Goggles will drink from the toilet, standing on her withered haunches until she is sated and then she'll belch water onto the floor so that tiny Gizzard can lap the liquid of life. But Goggles as savior of Gizzard is the dream of a romantic fool. I see now Gizzard, my ancient Pekinese, is going to outlive her when I witness her haunches give out and she quivers on the dull, gray carpet. Her eyes will not reflect me. She shivers and curls up next to me curled up on the couch. I smudge her with sage and call the vet for the coup de grace, but the vet is out tending pigs. I get up and drive into Marshall for some new .12 gauge shells. When I get back an hour later, Goggles is stiff. Gizzard is asleep and he must have slept when the reaper came for Goggles. Outside, an inexorable sadness rises from the dead, blue soil and fouls my heart. I lie down on the rug and snuggle my dead little dog and try to remember something in the somewhere when young and strong, we were.

RYAN G. VAN CLEAVE

Adrienne Rich, or the Ninth Symphony of Beethoven Understood at Last as a Question of Faith

Perhaps it's the trombone's
haranguing throat, those deep
storm grumbles, or maybe
it's the controlled panic
of French horns, how the
air smacks of their desperate
measures—what I hear Ludwig
saying is that he is scared,
that fear floats like a hydrogen-
bloated blimp drifting close,
too close, to a radio tower. It's
everyone he loves examining
the sky as if they sense the air
raid siren is broken. Forget
all anachronisms, just forget
that Beethoven never jitterbugged
and would surely have buckled
before a pair of Celestions offering
Eminem, P-Diddy. What's worthy,
what's lasting, what matters
is that we seek Joy in every sober
mantel portrait, that the dust
jackets of great epics are smudged
often and eagerly, that even after
the euphoria of prayer-trumpets
wears off and traffic's running late
and the pavement is oozing with
slush and the ominous ozone shadow
looms overhead, we smile inwardly
at our transient souls and climb

through the day, always towards an
upper rung of Dante's, the high-wire
act of faith we sometimes forget to dare.

DOMINIC ALBANESE

Saturday Sunday Selections

near the end of another run
some bitter powder left

foolish hells angels pass
noisy
I remain remote
spending hours like
money
Dominic
such a beautiful
name

*

    at it again
        thought I put my wrenches
    away for good.
           but no, cash poor at loose ends
    back to the garage

high end iron
    gotta admit that
        used, abused, neglected
pays good. inspect, repair, fold and fondle
road test at will, rather fast too
    o mickey the mechanic
           da wife says yr a writer now
    this is just a paycheck
funny how my head is full of cars again
        greasemonkey wordsmith back at it again

*

trade money for hours
hours produced one bent finger at a time

*

the metal part
of my life
                stays active
                parts of my
                plant and
                water self
                        lack attention

why, I
                        wonder
                                were we shown
        so many ways
                        but given
                so little time

believe it
the power of the river
having traveled so very far
to get here
even if only to pass
                        wild flowers a riot of color on the hill at sunset

*

my old life
don't haunt me no more
it even makes me laugh
what a dolt
tore up from the floor up
locked in a cell
cheat steal slip slide scam
all those days away

between AA and the woman
I married
better times now
all praise to God
who in the highest
made so visible
what I never saw before
stillness
shadows
softness
light
joy
gladness
even the hour of death

WALTER PAVLICH

Letter to Jerry

In a message dated 5/7/02 10:32:08 PM Pacific Daylight Time, Walter Pavlich, artguy@mac.com, writes to fish decoy carver Jerry Matzen:

Hi Jerry,

I get the infamous writer's block from time to time. It's no fun and very frustrating. One thing I've learned is that in order to write my good poems, I have to write my bad ones. In other words, just keep my finger in the pot and something will begin to appear. Is there a decoy you've always wanted to try? Ever thought of doing a version of the first decoy you've ever done? Or two fish that Noah would have put on the ark? Or a fish that lives all alone at the bottom of the sea? Or different parts of different fishes to make just one fish? Or a fish that God started, but didn't finish it because he got distracted making other animals. I don't know where you start on a decoy, but you could try starting on a decoy in a place you've never started on.... just some ideas.... Or a fish whose desire is to eat the entire world......now, you've really got me going..... a fish that's more like a bird than a fish..... a very sad fish who had suffered a great loss...... a fish who knows all that there is to know and then some..... a fish who has just had the idea to walk up on the sand..... a fish with the happiest colors but who has never seen itself in a mirror.....I'll stop here.....ask me again tomorrow and I'll have some other Walt ideas....

Many blessings to you my pal,

Walt

Jerry Matzen

CLARENCE MAJOR

The Poet's Villa

We visited the poet's house—
a stone villa five hundred years standing,
way out in the countryside, still,
the place of his travail.
Three caretakers, men all, said
everything was as he left it—lace,
even soap in dish,
slippers by bed,
graceful chairs,
and one said at night he saw
the poet's face still reflected
in the hall mirror.

In his poems the poet understands:
his own hands, his own pace and toil,
his brother's life, his mother's loss,
the poet understands sky and river.
He undertakes them all.

And in the boarding school photograph
we found among school records,
his little boy-arms crossed as if to say
I am not here—I've already moved on.

People in the village said
he would never amount to anything.
The photo though shows
who he will become—look at those eyes!

And we came out onto the landing
of the poet's villa
and stood on the stone steps,
looking out across the valley,
and saw that the sun was still high,
and we had lots of light left.

Douglas Blazek

A Good Growl for God at Walter's Wake

Few experiences teach.
But that's not their fault. A poet's
fingers. Quick bent. And
the snap is done.
One moment against the next
until what suffices for pleasure
is gone.
My life. Your life. But
not the poem.
Not that unending lightning strike
against
the dark brass of night.
The hardest things the heart
can do
tapped against its bell.
A beast come pulsing
into beauty's vision
vibrating loud
between
my eyes. A good
growl for god. Makes
me awake this time.
This time in the teaching
that has yet to stop.

James DenBoer

Watching Eagles

Madder than mushrooms,
sharper than grass—where's the one
I used to be—younger than birds?

There's no asking that
isn't an answer.

The rubbing stones make dust,
the wind rubs shapes in the sand.

There's no guess that
can't be wrong.

Give me back twenty years
and I will walk to Great Slave Lake
to watch the eagles.

Or take me back to sit
next to my grandfather
in his striped canvas deck chair
and I might listen.

Fill my pail with the blackberries
that have made these stains
on my fingers.

Don't tell me what you don't know.

Let me sleep past five a.m.
Let me read past midnight.
I will write a better book than that one.
Singing lifted me up
to now.

I was serious as an old horse,
crazier than a hospital,
then; I was black-haired as a dog.

Don't make me dream
that dream again.

JACK MARSHALL

Re-entry

When I come back from the starry spheres
preserved in the molecules within us and am greeted
in my descent by the creamy sight

of a café au lait face glancing up from under
a green-tinted windshield passing beneath
cypress and pines in the deepening pinks and mauves

presiding over permanent sunset, and I happen
to catch sight of the last rays concentrated in the lens
of a single window before it loses its brilliance

to slow darkness; or in dawn birdsong, fog
spun of fine tulle rising out of an earth itself gazing
upward at a gradually brightening sky, I want to mingle

with the dew on the grasses, those early evaporating
clues I would otherwise whizz by. For now they leave me
as usual no wiser but with a sinking feeling

as when falling into a petrifaction
profound as an absolute that grips
like alien beings who telepathically order: leave

your losses or else see them added to the sheer
crushing weight of accumulated regret
which even as you speak rises

to sink you. As evening grows darker,
and moonlight brighter, and heavier the dews,
and each magnified bead's portion of the sky

beamed down upon the earth leaves
its brief
brightness there, when I return

I wouldn't change a thing, let alone my life.

JAMES LEE JOBE

Potato Bug Feet

At bedtime my son and I talk to the moon and say
a tiny prayer. How tiny? Smaller than Potato Bug feet.

WALTER PAVLICH

The Weight of a Flame

There is only one fire.
It has been passed from place
to place like a sprinter's baton.

You cannot touch fire—
only your own burnt hand.
Blisters choose their own pain,

filling with water from a clear sea.
And don't try kicking the light
or the brilliant heat.

It provokes Fervor,
the god of flame,
whose insistence seems

flattering at first:
it is not the cigarette
he puts to your lips,

but the match.
His teeth stink.
The coffee's never hot

enough and he would eat
you in front of yourself
the way a crow partakes

of the living eye
of a mostly dead jay.
But fire gently boils

a bear from the inside,
all froth. As a chimney anchors
the memory of the house

against the exact weight of flame.

Because of your melodic nature,
the moonlight
never misses an appointment.

—Chinese fortune cookie

In Fond
Rembrance
of my kind
Friend
"Walter
Paulich

Jerry Matzen

Contributors

Dominic Albanese (Oak Grove, OR) is "Brooklyn born, Viet Nam raised from career criminal to church gardener in 58 years. Happy to be a grandfather." His poems are "published to help others help themselves."

Francisco Aragón (Elkhart, IN), author of *Puerta del Sol* (Bilingual Press, forthcoming), is co-editing an anthology based on The Chicano Chapbook Series. Founder of Momotombo Press, he is an editorial consultant at the Institute for Latino Studies, University of Notre Dame.

The most recent books by **Marvin Bell** (Iowa City, IA & Port Townsend, WA) are *Rampant* (2004), *Nightworks: Poems 1962-2000, Poetry for a Midsummer's Night* (1998), *Wednesday* (1998), *Ardor: The Book of the Dead Man, Vol. 2* (1997), *The Book of the Dead Man* (1994), *A Marvin Bell Reader: Selected Poetry and Prose* (1994), and *Iris of Creation* (1990). Bell is the longest-serving professor in the University of Iowa Writers' Workshop, having been there since 1965, and is the first Poet Laureate of Iowa.

Doug Blazek (Sacramento, CA) is the author of many books of poetry and his work has appeared recently in *The Seattle Review, Hayden's Ferry Review,* and *The Sacramento Anthology.*

Playwright **Lee Blessing** (NYC, NY) was nominated for a Tony Award and a Pulitzer Prize for *A Walk in the Woods* (1987). His work has been frequently produced in regional theaters. *Thief River* is a story, told over three generations, about the lifelong, largely unrequited love affair of two men from a Minnesota farming community.

John Allen Cann (Sacramento, CA) writes, "For the last 25 years I've been fortunate that my modest livelihood has come from engaging the young with poetry—for this I am truly grateful—as I am increasingly for my work early on at Cornell with poets A.R. Ammons and Bill Matthews."

Eduardo C. Corral (Casa Grande, AZ) holds degrees from Arizona State University and the Iowa Writers' Workshop; his poems have appeared in *Black Warrior Review, Colorado Review, Indiana Review*, and *www.versedaily.com*.

James DenBoer (Sacramento, CA) is a bookseller (www.paperwrk.com), author of two books with University of Pittsburgh Press, several chapbooks, and recipient of grants and awards from the NEA, PEN/New York, Author's League, and others.

Joseph Duemer (Potsdam, NY) has published three collections of poetry, most recently *Magical Thinking* (Ohio State University), is poetry editor of *The Wallace Stevens Journal*, and had a Fulbright to Hanoi, where he translated Vietnamese poets. He teaches at Clarkson University.

Gene Epstein (NYC, NY) was born in 1927; his first short story appeared in *Best American Short Stories of 1965*. He and his wife are proprietors of Epstein/Powell Gallery of Outsider Art.

Alejandro Escudé (Davis, CA), originally from Argentina, tells the story of immigrating to the U.S. in his sonnet sequence, from which this selection is taken. He is a teacher, translator, social/political thinker, and graduate of the UC Davis Creative Writing Masters program.

John Olivares Espinoza (Tempe, AZ) is the author of *Aluminum Times* (Swan Scythe Press, 2002); his work also appears in *So Luminous the Wildflowers: An Anthology of California Poets* and *Under the Fifth Sun: Latino Literature from California*. He is a Soros New American Fellow at Arizona State University.

Jeffrey Franklin (Denver, CO) teaches at the University of Colorado at Denver and serves as poetry editor of the *North Carolina Literary Review*; his poems have appeared in The *Hudson Review, New England Review, Shenandoah, Third Coast*, as well as in the 2002 *Best American Poetry*.

Arthur Ginsberg (Seattle, WA), winner of the William Stafford Award for Washington State, 2003, is a neurologist, whose poems appear in *Blood and Bone* (University of Iowa Press).

Joseph Green (Longview, WA) won the Floating Bridge Press Poetry Chapbook Award in 2001 for *The End of Forgiveness*. He has held a writing residency at Fundación Valparaíso, in Mojácar, Spain, where "Among the Potshards" takes place.

Eric Gudas (Pasadena, CA) is the author of *Beautiful Monster* (Swan Scythe Press, 2003); his poems, essays, and literary interviews have appeared in such publications as *The American Poetry Review, Crazyhorse, The Iowa Review,* and *Poetry Flash.*

Arthur Heehler (Davis, CA), Chicago-born, arrived in California in 1974, farmed, bee-keeped, wrote poetry, taught school, and photographed the landscape.

W. Joe Hoppe (Austin, TX) Hoppe was awarded a James A. Michener postgraduate fellowship from the Texas Center for Writers in 1995 and wisely used the time and funds to be a house-dad to his newborn son Max. Nowadays he picks up Max after school and teaches at Austin Community College.

James Lee Jobe (Davis, CA) has published three chapbooks of poetry and is a Sacramento radio D.J.

Harold Johnson (Portland, OR) is a teacher, editor, writer of poems and fiction, and fellow of the USA-Africa project of the Ragdale Foundation of Lake Forest, Illinois.

Adrian C. Louis (Marshall, MN) is the author of many collections of poetry and prose: *Bone & Juice; Ancient Acid Flashes Back; Ceremonies of the Damned; Vortex of Indian Fevers; Blood Thirsty Savages; Days of Obsidian, Days of Grace; Among the Dog Eaters; Fire Water World; Wild Indians & Other Creatures; Skins: A Novel.* He claims to have been "once a studly and often loutish man [who] now swims in the tepid sea of middle age."

C.G. Macdonald (Davis, CA) has published poems widely, in journals including *Reed, Texas Review* and *Western Humanities Review*. His most recent awards include the 2000 Bazanella Poetry Prize from CSUS, and the 2002 Carpenter Prize from *The Lyric*.

Clarence Major (Davis, CA) was nominated for the 1999 National Book Award in poetry for *Configurations: New and Selected Poems 1958-1998* (Copper Canyon, 1999). Besides his many novels, non-fiction, and poetry collections, he is editor of *The Garden Thrives: Twentieth Century African-American Poetry* (Harper Collins, 1996), *Juba to Jive: A Dictionary of African-American Slang* (Viking, 1994), and *Calling the Wind: Twentieth Century African-American Short Stories* (Harper Collins, 1993). His latest book of poems is *Waiting for Sweet Betty* (Copper Canyon, 2002).

Jack Marshall (El Cerrito, CA) most recently published *Gorgeous Chaos: New and Selected Poems 1965-2001*(Coffee House Press). His *Sesame* won a PEN Center West Literary Award and was a National Book Critics Circle Award finalist.

Jerry Matzen (Long Beach, WA) is featured in *Fish Decoy Makers Past and Present* by Donald J. Peterson. In Nevis, MN, he ran Jerry's Bait Shop and liked to spear on West Crooked Lake. His carvings are much sought after and admired.

Ron Mohring (Lewisburg, PA) teaches literature and creative writing at Bucknell University, where he is Senior Associate Editor of *West Branch*. His three chapbooks are *Amateur Grief, The David Museum*, and *Beneficence*.

Larry Moffi (Silver Spring, MD) is the author of three collections of poems including *A Citizen's Handbook: Poems* and *A Simple Progression*. He is a baseball historian, author of *This Side of Cooperstown: An Oral History of Major League Baseball in the 1950s* and *Crossing the Line: Black Major Leaguers, 1947-1959*.

Of **Walter Pavlich** (1955-2002) Gary Snyder wrote, "These poems [in *The Spirit of Blue Ink*] are sheer enjoyment of mind to read, magically plain, centered, bending and opening things. Here are new words, new uses." Walter has a role in the last few minutes of the film *River's Edge*.

Jack Ridl (Holland, MI) was named Michigan Professor of the Year in 1996 by the Carnegie Foundation; he lives with his wife Julie along Lake Michigan, where he feeds lots of birds.

David Salner (Frederick, MD) has worked in iron ore mines, foundries, machine shops, and walked picket lines all over the country; his first collection, *The Chosen*, was published by Pudding House; poems appear in *Threepenny Review* and *Prairie Schooner*.

Lewis Smith (1907-1998) was included in a museum show on art brut in France in 2000 and in the exhibition "ABCD: une collection d'art brut," touring the U.S. in 2002-3. Most of his life he lived in the woods of Ohio, drawing, writing, and painting on paper, cardboard, the walls of his house and on buildings. His work reflects his preoccupation with muscular women, trains, time, and money. He took up art in his 60s.

Adam Soldofsky (Davis, CA) was born in 1981 in Oakland, CA; he is a prize winning poet, author of the chapbook *My Father's Books* and founder of Apple Core Press.

George Vahle (La Mesa, CA) is a free lance writer and marketing consultant. His poem "The Signs All Around Me" won first place in the San Diego Writers' Cooperative contest, 2003.

Ryan G. Van Cleave (Green Bay, WI) is author of *Like Thunder: Poets Respond to Violence in America* and *Contemporary American Poetry: Behind the Scenes*.

Randy White (Rocklin, CA) is the author of *Motherlode/La Veta Madre* (Blue Oak/Capra Press, 1977); his work has appeared in the *Range of Light Anthology, Sulfur, Sierra Journal, Calaveras Station,* and other magazines.

ACKNOWLEDGMENTS

All poems are printed here for the first time, copyright © 2003 in their authors' names, with permission of their authors, or are reprinted with permission from the following sources:

Marvin Bell, "He Said To" and "The Uniform" from *Nightworks: Poems 1962-2000;* copyright © by Marvin Bell; reprinted with the permission of Copper Canyon Press, P.O. Box 271, Port Townsend, WA 98368-0271; Eduardo Corral's "Acquired Immune Deficiency Syndrome" first appeared in *Indiana Review;* "Celestial Woman Undressed by a Monkey," copyright © 2000 by Joseph Duemer; grateful acknowledgment is made to *Common Ground Review,* in which an earlier version of Jeffrey Franklin's "Julian Bream" appeared; W. Joe Hoppe's "Sanding Floors" was originally published in *Borderlands Texas Poetry Review;* Harold Johnson's "At the Jackson Pollock Retrospective in L.A." was published in *Fireweed: Poetry of Western Oregon* and in Peter Sears' and Michael Malan's anthology *Millenial Spring: Eight New Oregon Poets;* Jack Marshall's "Re-entry" is reprinted from *Gorgeous Chaos: New and Selected Poems 1965-2001,* copyright © 2002 by Jack Marshall; reprinted with the permission of the author and Coffee House Press, Minneapolis, Minnesota; Larry Moffi's "Wolf Whistle" first appeared in *Poetry;* "PGH Airport" and "Windows" appeared first in *The David Museum,* New Michigan Press, copyright © by Ron Mohring, reprinted by permission of the poet; Jack Ridl's "The Man Who Wants to Change the World" appeared first in *Against Elegies,* The Center for Book Arts, NYC; we would like to thank the editors of *The Baltimore Review* for permission to reprint David Salner's "The Machinist and the Cell Phone"; permission is granted by Matt Lippa, Artisans, for reproduction of both sides of the drawing by Lewis Smith ("Any number becomes 1" and "Putting apple sauce on a mortgage") for the purpose of use in *How To Be This Man,* Swan Scythe Press, the Walter Pavlich Memorial Prize; Randy White's "Fishing the Klamath River, 1953" previously appeared in *Poetry Now: Sacramento's Literary Review.*